Just A Zillion Things Before you Go

Written by

HUGH O'NEILL

Illustrated by

DAVE CHISHOLM

JUST A ZILLION THINGS BEFORE YOU GO

Written by Hugh O'Neill
Illustrated by Dave Chisholm

Edited by Josh O'Neill
Designed by Maëlle Doliveux

First edition, 2021. Printed in China. ISBN: 978-1-94-888627-7

To:_____

From: _____

Hey! What's with the suitcase? You going somewhere?

You taking a trip? Is that farewell in the air?

What's that you say? You're leaving the nest?

You're about to embark on the rest of your quest?

Quit kidding around! Stop stuffing that sack!

What possible reason could a kid have to pack?

You may not have noticed, but you're still just a child,

And a young cub like you won't be safe in the wild.

Well, yes, you're correct. You do *look* strong and grown,

But that doesn't mean you can be on your own,

Don't be silly, sweetheart. You're nowhere near ready.

Why only last week you bit that boy Teddy.

What do you mean that was *twelve* years ago?!!!

No! No! No! No! No! No! No! No! No! No! No!

Hmm... just checked the records, it looks like you're right,

You appear to have gone and grown up overnight,

Whew! That was fast! Childhood done in a blink!

That zipped by a little too quick, don't you think?

But alright, that's cool! Look at us! Switching gears!

Need help with the packing? No, no, those aren't tears!

We're excited for you! You're gonna do great!

Sure, we'll miss you a lot. But the future won't wait.

You'll need a sweater or two, some undies and socks,

Maybe toothpaste and floss to toss in that box,

A bathrobe, some scissors, a mirror to look in,

A nail-clipper, hairbrush and a pot you might cook in.

And just so you don't get perplexed or kerfuffled,

You might want some wisdom to cram in your duffel.

We'd intended, dear kid, to share tons of stuff,

About flowers and engines and when you should bluff,

About driving and swimming and food and good health,

About finding true love and amassing great wealth.

You may well have noticed our plan hasn't worked out,

We've shared almost nothing about whittling or grout,

Or plumbing or dancing or cooking or thrift,

Or staying on course if your boat starts to drift.

We got kinda busy what with earning a living.

And amid all the laughs, we forgot wisdom-giving.

Now you're leaving home without the stuff that we know,

About sewing and rowing, and how to save dough,

About hope, about hearts, about protein and passion,

About fishing and fiber, faith, fruit, fear and fashion.

One thing we did right was give safety advice,

But when we warned you of dangers, you weren't so nice,

You mocked our concerns from the time you were small,

And you paid... let's be frank... no attention at all,

We don't *like* being worried, it's not something we *choose*,

But when you've got something precious, there's so much to lose.

When we had you at home we could ouch-proof your life,

But out there in the world?! Yikes! The edge of a knife!

Out there you'll face risks, some soon, others later,

Bugs that might sting you, an occasional 'gator.

There are boo-boos and ow-ies and tigers and snakes,

Tornadoes and germs! Now and then, 'quakes!

But now that you're leaving, enough riffs of dread!

Let's toast the adventures taking shape in your head.

And oh, by the way, we've got last second advice,

Some out-the-door wisdom that will give your life spice.

But because you've been fresh, you'll have to wait a few stanzas,

To hear the one thought that makes life a bonanza,

And in payback for the mocking that fell from your lips?

Even though you don't want them - some *more* driving tips!

Check the tread monthly on all of your tires,

And drive so that no sudden moves are required,

To avoid fender-benders, here's a great rule of thumb:

Assume the guy up-ahead will do something dumb.

Okay, enough cautions, oh, precious young one,

How 'bout some fun facts 'bout the big, yellow sun?

It warms up our faces and lights up our ways,

But behind all that shining, lurk bad UV rays.

Okay! Okay! We'll stop with the warnings,

If you promise to do a few things every morning,

Slather on sunscreen, maybe don a big hat,

And cover all parts — whether bony or fat,

And if you live way up high, say in west Colorad-uh,

It's hard to apply as much goop as you oughta.

But wait! Enough worry! There's cheering to do!

But first, before that, a list of things to eschew,

Eschew? Fancy word that means to *steer clear of*,

And there are a few things that you should have some fear of.

Eschew scary caves! Eschew NASCAR dreams!!

Eschew candles and pit bulls! Eschew trampolines!

And be wary of folks who say *bungee* or *summit*,

Since humans like these tend to leap and to plummet.

There are so many risks, no mere mortal could list 'em.

But brace yourself, kid, for a shock to your system,

The worst thing of all that could happen to you?

The risk of all risks? Taking too few.

Surprised you with that one...but yup, you heard right!

Maybe, just maybe, we're not so uptight.

See, when you were a kid, you were one reckless bear,

So it only made sense that we had to preach care,

Your urge to be head-long and rash was hard-wired,

So a dollop of caution was what was required.

But now that we've put some *beware* in your brain,

We owe you some good news before you get on that train.

You're prob'ly entitled to both halves of the story,

Sure, the world has its perils, but wow, it's got glory!

Any fool can be *safe* — just don't leave the house!

Any rodent can go through the world like a mouse,

But that's not for you. You want to live big and free,

Ships are safe in the harbor, but they should be at sea.

Now by *sea*, we don't mean … well, actual water.

That's not a safe spot for beloved son or daughter.

No, *at sea*, means engaged, involved in the game,

On land, nice and dry, but hey, making some waves!

You'll have to be careful, but brave is good too.

To have a sweet life, that's the mixture for you,

If you're *only* courageous, you might get injured or gored,

But if you're *only* careful, you will surely get bored.

So, stretch limits, child. Be sure you're failing enough,
Comfort zones are cozy, but don't teach you much.
And hey! Want some wisdom as sage as the Buddha's?
Go out on limb. Why? That's where the fruit is.

Don't be fearful of flopping. You'll hit some rough weather,

But failures are fleeting, and success is forever,

Losses aren't losses if they show you some truth,

Sadness carves space where wisdom takes root.

So be bold *and* be timid, be sheepish *and* strong,

Sometimes raise your voice, but then sing a soft song.

Play offense *and* defense. Give a lot. Sometimes take,

Hit the gas hard, *as* you're riding the brake.

THE FUN WAY!

THE SAFE WAY

If you want it all simple, seek some other world,

Not this wonderful puzzle into which you've been hurled.

If the games were all easy, hey, that's minor league!

Here on earth, things are tricky. Yea! That's the intrigue!

Life is a challenge. But it's also a lark,

A test of your mettle and a walk in the park.

Some rough and some smooth will be waiting for you,

Life can be salty, but it's sugary too.

If you've got any interest in love or in wealth,

Then get in the game, get yourself off the shelf.

Don't sit on the sidelines, chilled by your fears,

Don't wait 'til you're ready. Heck, that could take years!

Dive in! — check the depth first — just be sure to get wet!

Don't sit around fretting, don't hedge every bet,

Throw lots of good stuff in this cake you are baking,

'Cause you miss all of the shots that you don't wind up taking.

Don't find excuses, and don't temporize.
Step one is Engage. Step two: Improvise.
Spread your arms wide, whatever the cost,
Life can't hand you gifts if you keep your arms crossed.

We've cherished it all! Oh, how the years flew!
And though you're a wise guy, we loved tending you,
If you settle in Brooklyn or migrate to Rome,
Wherever *we* are, you can call that place home.
Call when you're happy. And call if you're blue,
Your fights are our fights. Your pals are ours, too.

So, be careful, be careful, and then careful some more,

And then stop being careful, and charge out the door,

That's life you hear calling from over the hill,

Come hither, it whispers, I'll give you some thrills.

So, cast off the bowlines! With your toothbrush, go nuts!

Head into the jungle! Disinfect paper cuts!

If you'd like to know something, take Step One to learn it,

You deserve all the best. But hey, gotta earn it!

If you're as prudent and cautious as you are daring and bold,

You'll find buried treasure and live to get old.

Your days will be chewy, your regrets teeny-tiny,

You'll be at home in the world; your life will be shiny.

Oh, don't drive when you're angry. And true love is mighty.

And this could be handy: lefty-loosey, righty-tightey.

And keep this in mind as you head out the door,

First take some precautions, then, go forward full bore.

You could sport a helmet wherever you go,

Not just when you're biking or skiing on snow,

Just think of a helmet as a fortified hat,

That you wear when you shower, drink coffee or nap.

Okay, grown-up child, maybe *this* goes too far,

But maybe you'll wear one while driving a car.

Taking care of yourself makes you fully-equipped,

With a belt *and* suspenders you can safely take risks.

So-long, darling cub. No, no ... we're not sad,

Our hearts are near bursting, but that makes us glad.

No really, it does. We're inspired by your arc.

Take care of yourself. Blow on your spark.

Turns out there are only two things you need know.

First, strap on your helmet, then...